The GOLDEN THREAD

Words of wisdom for a changing world

Compiled with
calligraphy & illustration
by

Dorothy Boux

Shepheard~Walwyn   &   Gateway Books
London   Bath

First published in 1990
by GATEWAY BOOKS
The Hollies, Wellow,
Bath BA2 8QJ

in association with

SHEPHEARD-WALWYN (Publishers) Ltd
26, Charing Cross Road
London WC2HODH

©1990 Dorothy Boux

No part of this book may be reproduced
in any form without prior permission
from the publisher, except for the quotation
of brief passages in criticism.

Calligraphy and paintings by Dorothy Boux
Printed and bound by
Mandarin Offset Ltd
Hong Kong & London
Cover design by John Douet

British Library Cataloguing in Publication Data:
The Golden thread: words of hope for a changing world.
   1. Life - Philosophical perspectives
   I. Boux, Dorothy
   128
   ISBN 0-946551-65-0

TABLE OF CONTENTS

Life's journey is a pageant which reveals itself from moment to moment as each step discloses a facet of the one great unity.

The uncharted land stretches ahead, offering a bewildering variety of paths. Some of us choose the highways, others the lanes and footpaths, but in reality we are all travelling together and sooner or later will reach our single destination; for all races, nations and religions combine in a chord based upon one keynote, our common humanity, which holds us in a single bond of harmony.

The profound questions of life and death present themselves to heart and mind, as each of us strives to discover, within the apparent diversity, the eternal and unchanging source of life.

As one great poet said 'Between our birth and death we may touch understanding, as a moth brushes a window with its wing'. This great life cycle lies at the root of this book, but also interweaves with the

familiar measure of the day, from the stillness just before the dawn to the tranquillity of the fading light of evening. Reflecting each other, the day and the life slip by; the morning yields to the maturity of later noon before bowing to the peace of the evening, whilst, like an explorer in an unknown land, the individual strives to connect with an inner thread of wisdom, common to all.

This inner quest to unite with a spiritual reality leads us to a fount of wisdom where the great teachings and lesser voices combine to point the way. On such a scale individual limitations fall into place. One had only to remember that the role of the scribe is to record faithfully, drawing upon the inspiration of colour and form to feel at one with greater practitioners, and in all humility echo these words:

'I am a late-come scribe, who loves the Master and his love of men, and tell this legend, knowing he was wise....'

May this book bring you to peace.

Dorothy Boux, 1990.

ACKNOWLEDGEMENTS

'When you work you are a flute through whose heart the whispering of the hours turns to music. Which of you would be a reed, dumb and silent, when all else sings together in unison?' These words by Kahlil Gibran took on new meaning during the writing of this book, when the pen became an instrument which transmitted the wisdom of past voices, and I joyfully acknowledge those men and women whose thoughts gave constant inspiration and whose vision became the fabric of the work.

Thanks are also due to Millicent Harris for the prayer from Iona, Charles Garnet for the prose by Henry Scott-Holland, Mervyn Goff for two oriental pieces, and the unknown Scandinavian lady who collected and sent quotations.

A special thanks to Sir George Trevelyan whose book *Magic Casements* gave inspiration at a particularly difficult time, and to Joan Crammond and Sheila Rosenberg for their advice and support.

My gratitude to Arthur Farndell and David Warner for their meticulous checking, and to Eliane Wilson for her sustaining encouragement.

To A.E.I. Falconar, my thanks for allowing quotes from his book *Gardens of Meditation* to be used, and to Anthony Hentschel for permission to use his poem. Also to the School of Economic Science and Shepheard-Walwyn Publishers, for permission to quote from *The Letters of Marsilio Ficino*.

For permission to include copyright material we gratefully acknowledge the following copyright holders:

Gerald Duckworth and Co. Ltd. for two verses from *All Things Considered* by Paul Roche.

Faber and Faber Ltd for lines from *The Ten Principal Upanishads*

translated by Shree Purohit Swami and W. B. Yeats and for
'Prayer Before Birth' from *Selected Poems* by Louis MacNeice.
Oxford University Press for two excerpts from *A Sleep of Prisoners*
by Christopher Fry (1951).
The Society of Authors as the literary representative of the Estates
of John Masefield for extracts from 'Laugh and be Merry' and 'Seekers'
and of Richard le Gallienne for an extract from *The More Excellent Way*.
Jonathan Cape Ltd, London and Henry Holt and Co Inc, New York on
behalf of the Estate of Robert Frost for the extract from 'Trial by
Existence' from *The Poetry of Robert Frost* edited by Edward Connery
Lathem, ©1934, ©1969 by Holt, Rinehart & Winston ©1962 by Robert Frost.
Sidgwick and Jackson Ltd for the extract from 'Ducks' by F. W. Harvey.
Macmillan Accounts and Administration Ltd for extracts from *Gitanjali*
by Rabindranath Tagore.
Krishnamurti Foundation Trust Ltd, Brockwood Park, Bramdean,
Hampshire, England for extracts from *The Only Revolution* by
J. Krishnamurti.
Penguin Books Ltd, London and Triangle Editions Inc, New York for
extracts from *Meetings with Remarkable Men* by G. I. Gurdjieff (Arkana,
1985) © Editions Janus, 1963.
Society of Metaphysicians, Hastings for an extract from the work
of Ralph Waldo Trine.
Whiteknights Press for 'Daydream' from *The Collected Poems of*
A. S. J. Tessimond, with translations by Jacques Prévert, edited by Hubert
Nicholson, 1986.
Aquilla Publishing U.K. Ltd, for an extract from *Obras Completas* of
Juan Ramon Jimenez translated by J. C. R. Green.
Anthony Sheil Associates Ltd on behalf of the Estate of Minnie
Louise Haskins for 'The Gate of the Year'.
The publisher has made every effort to trace copyright owners.
Where we have failed we offer our apologies and undertake to make
proper acknowledgement in reprints.

Could we with ink the ocean fill,
Were every blade of grass a quill,
Were the world of parchment made,
And every man a scribe by trade,
To write the love
Of God above
Would drain that ocean dry;
Nor would the scroll
Contain the whole
Though stretched from sky to sky.

MEIR BEN ISAAC NEHORAÏ

To fellow calligraphers ⁓

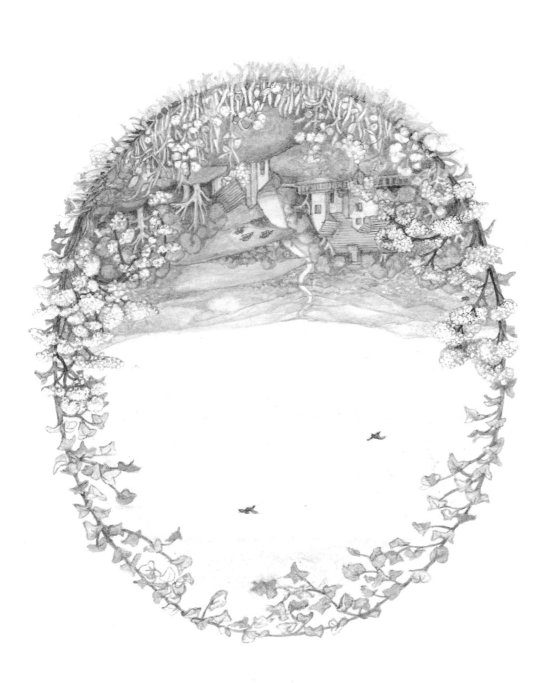

And from a clifftop is proclaimed
The gathering of the souls for birth....
And none are taken but who will,
Having first heard the life read out
That opens earthward, good and ill,
Beyond the shadow of a doubt;
And very beautifully God limns,
And tenderly, life's little dream,
But naught extenuates or dims,
Setting the thing that is supreme.

Nor is there wanting in the press
Some spirit to stand simply forth,
Heroic in its nakedness,
Against the uttermost of earth.
The tale of earth's unhonoured things
Sounds nobler there than 'neath the sun;
And the mind whirls and the heart sings,
And a shout greets the daring one...

And so the choice must be again,
But the last choice is still the same;
And the awe passes wonder then,
And a hush falls for all acclaim.
And God has taken a flower of gold
And broken it, and used therefrom
The mystic link to bind and hold
Spirit to matter till death come...

ROBERT FROST

1

THE SUN

wasn't up yet;
you could see the morning star
through the trees. There was a
silence that was really extraordinary.
Not the silence between two noises or
between two notes, but the silence that has
no reason whatsoever ~ the silence that
must have been at the beginning of the
world. It filled the whole valley and the hills.
The two big owls, calling to each other, never
disturbed that silence, and a distant dog
barking at the late moon was part of this
immensity. The dew was especially heavy,
and as the sun came up over the hill
it was sparkling with many colours
and with the glow which comes with
the sun's first rays...

Krishnamurti

AWAKE,

my heart, to be loved, awake, awake!
The darkness silvers away, the morn
doth break,
It leaps in the sky: unrisen lustres slake
The o'ertaken moon. Awake, O heart, awake...

Awake, the land is scattered with light,
and see,
Uncanopied sleep is flying from field
and tree:
And blossoming boughs of April in
laughter shake;
Awake, O heart, to be loved,
awake, awake!...

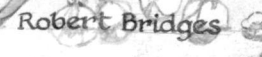
Robert Bridges

3

PRAYER·BEFORE·BIRTH

by Louis MacNeice

I AM NOT YET BORN,

O hear me.
Let not the bloodsucking bat or
the rat or the stoat or the club-
footed ghoul come near me.

I **AM** not yet born, console me.
I fear that the human race may with
tall walls wall me,
with strong drugs dope me,
with wise lies lure me, on black
racks rack me, in blood-baths roll me.

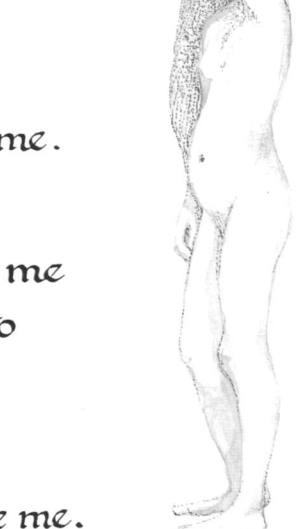

I **AM** not yet born; provide me
With water to dandle me, grass to
grow for me, trees to talk to me,
sky to sing to me,
birds and a white light
in the back of my mind to guide me.

I AM not yet born; forgive me
For the sins that in me the world
shall commit, my words when
they speak me, my thoughts
when they think me,
my treason engendered
by traitors beyond me,
my life when they murder by means of my
        hands, my death when they live me.

I AM not yet born; rehearse me
In the parts I must play and the cues I must
take when old men lecture me, bureaucrats
hector me, mountains frown at me, lovers
laugh at me, the white waves call me to folly
and the desert calls me to doom and the
beggar refuses my gift and my children curse me.

I AM not yet born; O hear me,
Let not the man who is beast or who thinks
        he is God come near me.

I AM NOT YET BORN,

O fill me
With strength against those who would freeze my
humanity, would dragoon me into a lethal
automaton, would make me a cog in a machine,
a thing with one face, a thing, and against all
those who would dissipate my entirety, would
blow me like thistledown hither and thither
or hither and thither like water held in the
hands would spill me.
Let them not make me a stone
and let them not spill me.

I was not
aware of the moment
when I first crossed the—
threshold of this life. What was
the power that made me open out
into this vast mystery like a bud
in the forest at midnight! When in
the morning I looked upon the light
I felt in a moment that I was no
stranger in this world, that the in-
scrutable without name and form
had taken me in its arms in the
form of my own mother.
Even so, in death the same
unknown will appear
as ever known to
me.
RABINDRANATH TAGORE

OUR BIRTH IS

but a sleep and a forgetting;
The soul that rises with us,
Our life's star,
Hath had elsewhere its setting,
And cometh from afar:
Not in entire forgetfulness,
And not in utter nakedness,
But trailing CLOUDS OF GLORY

do we come
From God, who is our HOME.

William Wordsworth

8

SHOOT,
FLAMING STARS.
Breakers, roar!
With polished jewels
of rock is laced the shore.
Winds, caress! Planets, spin!
The prize of greatest glory is ours to win.
Swan-moon rise! God-sun blaze!
A lady round with child fulfils her days.
Quiet feelings. Open heart.
The friend you make of silence cannot part.
Welcome shadows. Roads unwind.
The eyes that read these simple words
may they prove kind.
Sing cicadas! Prosper earth!
Each endless, vital moment is rebirth.
Shed old skin, serpent.
Find fresh wings, dove.
The art that made these
parts one whole you
know is love.

ANTHONY HENTSCHEL

9

HOSE undescribed, ambrosial mornings of summer, which I can remember, when a thousand birds were heard gently twittering and ushering in the light, like the argument to a new canto of an epic & heroic poem. The serenity, the infinite promise of such a morning. The song or twitter of the birds drips from the leaves like dew. Then there was something divine & immortal in our life. Henry Thoreau

WHEN you arise in the morning
Give thanks for the morning light.
Give thanks for your life and strength.
Give thanks for your food
And give thanks for the joy of living
And if perchance you see no reason
for giving thanks,
Rest assured the fault is in yourself.
N. American Indian

Hail to thee, blithe Spirit!
Bird thou never wert,
That from heaven, or near it
Pourest thy full heart
In profuse strains of unpremeditated art.

Higher still and higher
From the earth thou springest
Like a cloud of fire;
The deep blue thou wingest,
And singing still dost soar, and soaring
ever singest.

In the golden lightning
Of the sunken sun
O'er which clouds are brightening,
Thou dost float and run,
Like an unbodied joy whose race is just
begun.

P.B. Shelley ~

Thou art the sky and

O thou
beautiful,
there in the nest
it is thy love that
encloses the soul with
colours and sounds and
odours. There comes the
morning with the golden
basket in her right hand
bearing the wreath of beauty,
silently to crown the earth.
And there comes the evening over
the lonely meadows deserted by
herds, through trackless paths,

thou art the nest as well.

carry-
ing cool
draughts of peace
in her golden pitcher
from the western ocean
of rest.
But there, where spreads
the infinite sky for the soul
to take her flight in, reigns
the stainless white radiance.
There is no day nor night, nor
form nor colour, and never,
never a word.

RABINDRANATH TAGORE

RISE, O EARTH, FROM OUT THY SLUMBER,
FIELD OF THE CREATOR, ROUSE THEE,

Make the blade arise and flourish,
Let the stalks grow up and lengthen,
That the ears may grow by thousands,
Yet a hundredfold increasing,

By my ploughing and my sowing,

In return for all my labour...

KALEVALA ~ Finnish

THE MEADOWS ROLL AND
SWELL IN BILLOWY WAVES,
Bearing like a white-speckled foam
upon their crests
a sea of daisies
With here and there a floating patch
of crimson clover
or a golden haze of buttercups.

W. Hamilton Gibson

When God had finished the stars and whirl of
coloured suns
He turned His mind from big things to fashion
little ones,
Beautiful tiny things (like daisies) He made, and then
He made the comical ones in case the minds of men
Should stiffen and become
Dull, humourless and glum:
And so forgetful of their Maker be
As to take even themselves ~ quite seriously.
Caterpillars and cats are lively and excellent puns:
All God's jokes are good ~ even the practical ones!
And as for the duck, I think God must have
smiled a bit
Seeing those bright eyes blink on the day He
fashioned it.
And He's probably laughing still at the sound
that came out of its bill!

F. W. HARVEY

16

LAUGH

and be merry, remember, better the
world with a song,
Better the world with a blow in the
teeth of a wrong.
Laugh, for the time is brief, a thread
the length of a span.
Laugh, and be proud to belong to the
old proud pageant of man.

JOHN MASEFIELD

17

IN those vernal seasons of the year, when the air is calm and pleasant, it were an injury and a sullenness against Nature, not to go out and see her riches, and partake in her rejoicing with heaven and earth. John Milton.

18

THE whole
time in the open air,
resting at mid-day, under
the elms with the ripple of
heat flowing through the shadow;
at midnight between the ripe corn
and the hawthorne hedge on the
white camomile and the poppy pale
in the duskiness, with face upturned
to the thoughtful heaven. Consider
the glory of it, the life above this
life to be obtained from constant presence with the
sun-light and the
stars.

Richard Jefferies

19

I was utterly alone with the sun and the earth.
Lying down on the grass, I spoke in my soul to
the earth, the sun, the air, and the distant sea
far beyond sight. I thought of the earth's
firmness ~ I felt it bear me up; through the
grassy couch there came an influence as if
I could feel the great earth speaking to me.
I thought of the wandering air ~ its pureness,
which is its beauty; the air touched me and
gave me something of itself. I spoke to the

sea: though so far, in my mind I saw it, green at the rim of the earth and blue in deeper ocean... I turned to the blue heaven over, gazing into its depth, inhaling its exquisite colour and sweetness. The rich blue of the unattainable flower of the sky drew my soul towards it, and there it rested, for pure colour is rest of heart. By all these I prayed... Then, returning, I prayed by the sweet thyme, whose little flowers I touched with my hand; by the slender grass; by the crumble of dry chalky earth I took up and let fall through my fingers. Touching the crumble of earth, the blade of grass, the thyme flower, breathing the earth-encircling air, thinking of the sea and the sky, holding out my hand for the sunbeams to touch it, prone on the sward in token of deep reverence, thus I prayed . . .

Richard Jefferies. ~

I BELIEVE

in the deep blue sky and the smiling water.
I can see through the clouds of the sky and
am not afraid of the waves of the sea.

I BELIEVE

in the loving friendships given by the
flowers and the trees. Outwardly they die
but in the heart they live forever. Little
paths through the woods I love, and the
sound of leaves on the ground or of a nut
falling or even of a broken twig.

I BELIEVE

that the days to come already feel the
wonder of the days that are passed and will
permit the wonder to endure and increase.

I BELIEVE

in and love my belief in, and my love for,
all these things and most of all, I believe in
and love the Source of my belief and love.

ANCIENT CHINESE TRADITION

22

God is
in the water. God is
in the dry land, God is
in the heart.
God is in the forest, God is in
the mountain, God is in the cave.
God is in the earth, God is in
heaven...
Thou art in the tree, thou art
in its leaves,
Thou art in the earth,
thou art in the
firmament.

SIKH TRADITION

HELP ME

today to realise that you will be⟶
speaking to me through the events
of the day, through people, through
things, and through all creation.
Give me ears, eyes and heart to
perceive you, however veiled your
presence may be.
Give me insight to see through the
exterior of things to the interior
truth.
Give me your Spirit of discernment!
O Lord, thou knowest how busy I
must be this day.
If I forget thee, do not forget me !

JACOB ASTLEY

Look to this day for it is life;
the very life of life.
In its brief course lie all
the realities and truths of existence~
the joy of growth,
the splendour of action,
the glory of power.
For yesterday is but a memory,
And tomorrow is only a vision,
but today well lived makes every yesterday
a memory of happiness,
And every tomorrow a vision of hope.
Look well, therefore, to this day.

SANSKRIT HYMN

WHAT IS LIFE ?

It is the flash of a firefly in the night. It is the breath of a buffalo in the wintertime. It is the little shadow which runs across the grass and loses itself in the sunset.

CROWFOOT · N. AMERICAN INDIAN

26

LISTEN AGAIN

One evening at the
close of Ramazàn,
Ere the better Moon arose,
In that old Potter's shop I stood alone
With the Clay population round in rows.

And strange to tell, among the Earthen lot
Some could articulate, while others not:
And suddenly one more impatient cried~
'Who is the Potter, pray, and who the Pot?'

Then said another ~ 'Surely not in vain
My substance from the common Earth was ta'en
That He who subtly wrought me
into shape~
Should stamp me back to
common Earth again.'

RUBAIYAT ~ OMAR KHAYAM

27

SURELY

in the heavens and the earth
there are signs for the faithful:
in your own creation, and in the
beasts that are scattered far and
near, signs for true believers, in
the alternations of night and day,
in the sustenance Allah sends down
from heaven with which he revives
the earth after its death, and in
the marshalling of the winds,
signs for men of understanding.

THE KORAN

ASK NOW THE BEASTS,

and they shall teach thee; and
the fowls of the air, and they
shall tell thee : or speak to the
earth, and it shall teach thee;
and the fishes of the sea shall
declare unto thee.
Who knoweth not in all these
that the hand of the Lord hath
wrought this?
In whose hand is the soul of
every living thing, and the breath
of all mankind...

BOOK OF JOB

29

I passed along
the water's edge below
the humid trees,
My spirit rocked in evening light,
the rushes round my knees,
My spirit rocked in sleep and sighs;
and saw the moorfowl pace
All dripping on a grassy slope, and saw them
cease to chase
Each other round in circles, and heard the eldest
speak:
'Who holds the world between his bill and made us
strong or weak,
Is an undying moorfowl, and He lives beyond the sky.
The rains are from His dripping wing, the moonbeams
from His eye.'
I passed a little further on and heard a lotus talk:
'Who made the world and ruleth it, He hangeth
on a stalk.
For I am in His image made, and all this
tinkling tide
Is but
a sliding drop of rain
between His petals wide.'

A little way
within the gloom
a roebuck raised his eyes
Brimful of starlight, and he said:
'The Stamper of the Skies,
He is a gentle roebuck; for how else, I
pray, could He
Conceive a thing so sad and soft, a gentle thing
like me?'
I passed a little further on and heard a peacock say:
'Who made the grass and made the worms and made
my feathers gay,
He is a monstrous peacock, and He waveth all the night
His languid tail above us lit with myriad
spots of light.'

~ 'The Indian upon God' by W. B. Yeats

This
we know.
The earth does not belong
to man; man belongs to the
earth.
This we know.
All things are connected, like the
blood which unites one family.
All things are connected.
Whatever befalls the earth, befalls
the sons of the earth.
Man did not weave the web of
life; he is merely a strand in it.
Whatever he does to
the web, he does to
himself.
CHIEF SEATTLE ~ N. AMERICAN INDIAN

For the
absolute good is the
cause and source of all—
beauty, just as the sun is the
source of all daylight, and it cannot
therefore be spoken or written; yet we
speak and write of it, in order to start
and escort ourselves on the way, and
arouse our minds to the vision: like as
when one showeth a pilgrim on his way
to some shrine that he would visit:
for the teaching is only of whither
and how to go, the vision itself
is the work of him who hath
willed to see.

PLOTINUS

When I consider Thy heavens, the work of thy fingers, and the stars? which Thou hast ordained? The moon? What is man? And the son of man, that thou regardest him? that Thou art mindful of man, that Thou

WHAT IS MAN WHAT IS MAN WHAT IS MAN WHAT IS MAN WHAT IS MAN WHAT IS MAN

PSALM   EIGHT

The circular text reads: Behind the human face God was hiding • I did not know • I did not know • I veiled my eyes and separated from the truth

ISLAMIC

If all that exists in the world and in heaven is to be found in man, then what remains? God Himself has said in the scriptures, that He has made man in His own image. In other words, 'If you wish to see Me, I am to be found in man'. How thoughtless then on the part of man when, absorbed in his high ideals, he begins to condemn man, to look down upon man! However low and weak and sinful a man may be, there is yet the possibility of his rising higher than anything else in the whole of manifestation, whether on earth or in heaven; nothing else can reach the height which man is destined to reach. Therefore the point of view of the mystics and thinkers of all ages has always been reflected in their manner, which was a respectful attitude to all men.

HAZRAT INAYAT KHAN ~ SUFI

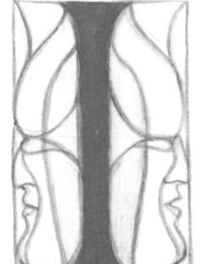see something of God each hour
of the twenty-four, and each
moment then,
In the faces of men and women I
see God, and in my own face
in the glass,
I find letters from God dropt in the street
and every one is signed by God's name,
And I leave them where they are, for I
know that whereso'ere I go,
Others will punctually come for ever and
ever.

WALT WHITMAN

he earth is but one country and
mankind its citizens.
Let not a man glory in this that
he loves his country, let him
rather glory in this that he loves his
kind.

BAHA'U'LLAH

THOUGH
A MAN
be soiled

With the sins of a
lifetime,
Let him but love me,
Rightly resolved,
In utter devotion:
I see no sinner,
That man
is holy.
Bhagavad - Gita ~

what if I do the opposite? What if I cheat and lie and steal, what injury will I do myself? Epictetus replied: No injury but that of not doing what you ought; you will destroy the man of fidelity in you, the man of honour, the man of decent behaviour. You need not look for greater injuries than these. You have been entrusted into your own keeping as if an orphan had been committed to your trust. God has delivered your own self into your keeping saying I had no one more faithful than you; Keep this man unchanged from the character with which nature endowed him—reverent, faithful, high-minded, undismayed, unimpassioned, unperturbed. After that do you so fail to keep him?

Epictetus

WHEN the human voyager has freed himself from his fears and accomplished all his physiological needs, it is as if he has climbed out of a deep pit and reached the top of a high hill from where he sees a vast land stretching in every direction. He is like a poor man lifted into a limitless inheritance. In this transcendent land are all manner of beauties, poetry and art and mysticism, and beyond are ideas and places of the brain that have not been explored or developed...

WHEN I started on my mental journey, the way seemed to be dark and impossible, yet I slowly found my way; and so can everyone else. I see the path to the peak experience as passing through the poetic, the emotional and the mystical regions. For the person who appreciates the beauty of poetry, the path through ecstasy and the peak experience is easy to see and it leads directly to the highest mysticism, ending in release and beyond. This is the way I know, and it is the only way I can write about but there are a hundred other ways to release and a hundred other ways for every intellect...

A.E.I. Falconar

The one
who sees all things
and yet rises above
them is the one who will
walk over the sea. No one
can reach the highest summits
of life, of wisdom, in a moment;
even a whole lifetime is too short.
Yet hope is necessary, for the
one who hopes and sees the
possibilities climbs towards the
summit, but the one who has no
hope has no legs to ascend
the hill of wisdom, the
summit of which is
the desired goal.

Hazrat Inayat Khan ~ Sufi ~

The hill, though high, I covet to ascend;
The difficulty will not me offend,
For I percieve the way to life lies here.
Come, pluck up heart let's neither
　　　　faint nor fear;
Better, though difficult, the right
　　　　way to go,
Than wrong, though easy,
Where the end is woe.

John Bunyan

Darest thou
now, O soul
Walk out with me
towards the unknown region
Where neither ground is for the
feet, nor any path to follow?

Prepare Thyself
for thou wilt have to
travel on alone.
The teacher can but point
the way. The path is one for
all, the means to reach the goal
must vary with the pilgrim.

Mme. Blavatsky

43

I AM THE WAY

Thou art the Way.
Hadst Thou been nothing but the goal,
I cannot say
If Thou hadst ever met my soul.

I cannot see ~
I, child of process ~ if there be
An end for me,
Full of repose, full of replies.

I'll not reproach
The road that winds, my feet that err.
Access, approach,
Art Thou, Time, Way, and Wayfarer.

Alice Meynell

44

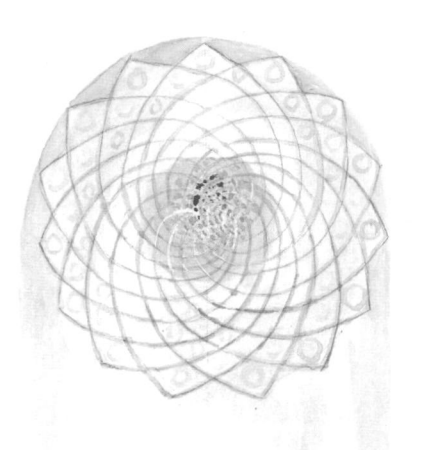

DEEP PEACE
of the Running Water to you.
DEEP PEACE
of the Flowing Air to you.
DEEP PEACE
of the Quiet Earth to you.
DEEP PEACE
of the Shining Stars to you.
DEEP PEACE
of the Son of Peace to you.

A Celtic Benediction

Good has no fear;
Good is itself, what ever comes.
It grows, and makes, and bravely
Persuades, beyond all tilt of wrong:
Stronger than anger, wiser than strategy,
Enough to subdue cities and men
If we believe it with a long courage of
truth.

Christopher Fry

Place, change, birth and death,
looked at down their deepest vistas, all
seem to me facets of a single idea: the
indestructibility of existence, a tissue
of fundamental relationships woven
into the garment without seam.

Paul Roche

I am a Lamp to thee who beholdest Me,
I am a Mirror to thee who perceivest Me,
I am a Door to thee who knockest at Me,
I am a Way to thee a wayfarer.

Hymn of Jesus   ~ Christian Tradition

And I said to the man
who stood at the
gate of the year:
'Give me a light that I may
tread safely into the
unknown'. And he replied:
'Go out into the darkness
and put your hand into
the hand of God . That
shall be to you better than
a light and safer than a
known way.

Minnie Louise Haskins

THERE IS NO SOLACE ON EARTH
for us ~ for such as we ~
Who search for a hidden city
that we shall never see.
Only the road and the dawn, the sun, the
wind, and the rain,
And the watch fire under stars, and sleep,
and the road again.
We seek the City of God, and the haunt
where beauty dwells,
And we find the noisy mart and the sound
of burial bells...
We travel from dawn to dusk, till the day
is past and by,
Seeking the Holy City beyond the rim of
the sky.
Friends and loves we have none, nor wealth
nor blest abode,
But the hope of the City of God at the
other end of the road.

John Masefield

I MET a traveller from an
antique land
Who said: Two vast and trunkless legs
of stone
Stand in the desert. Near them on the sand,
Half sunk, a shatter'd visage lies, whose frown
And wrinkled lip and sneer of cold command
Tell that its sculptor well those passions read
Which yet survive, stamp'd on these lifeless
things,
The hand that mock'd them and the heart
that fed;
And on the pedestal these words appear:
'My name is Ozymandias, king of kings:
Look on my works, ye Mighty, and despair!'
Nothing beside remains. Round the decay
Of that colossal wreck, boundless and bare,
The lone and level sands stretch far away.

P. B. Shelley.

ALAS,

the flowers last year so beautiful,
~ next year to be destroyed by frost;
so, too, will disappear this transient interlude,
a mere illusion.
The rainbow, so beautiful in all its hues,
fades away to nothingness;
so, too, will disappear these festive robes,
for all their finery.
However clear the voice and strong its echo,
it cannot last;
so, too, the mighty of this earth for all
their greatness.
Those who visit fairs and markets soon
disperse again;
so, too, our families, friends, and companions,
for all their number...

The Buddha's Law among
the Birds.

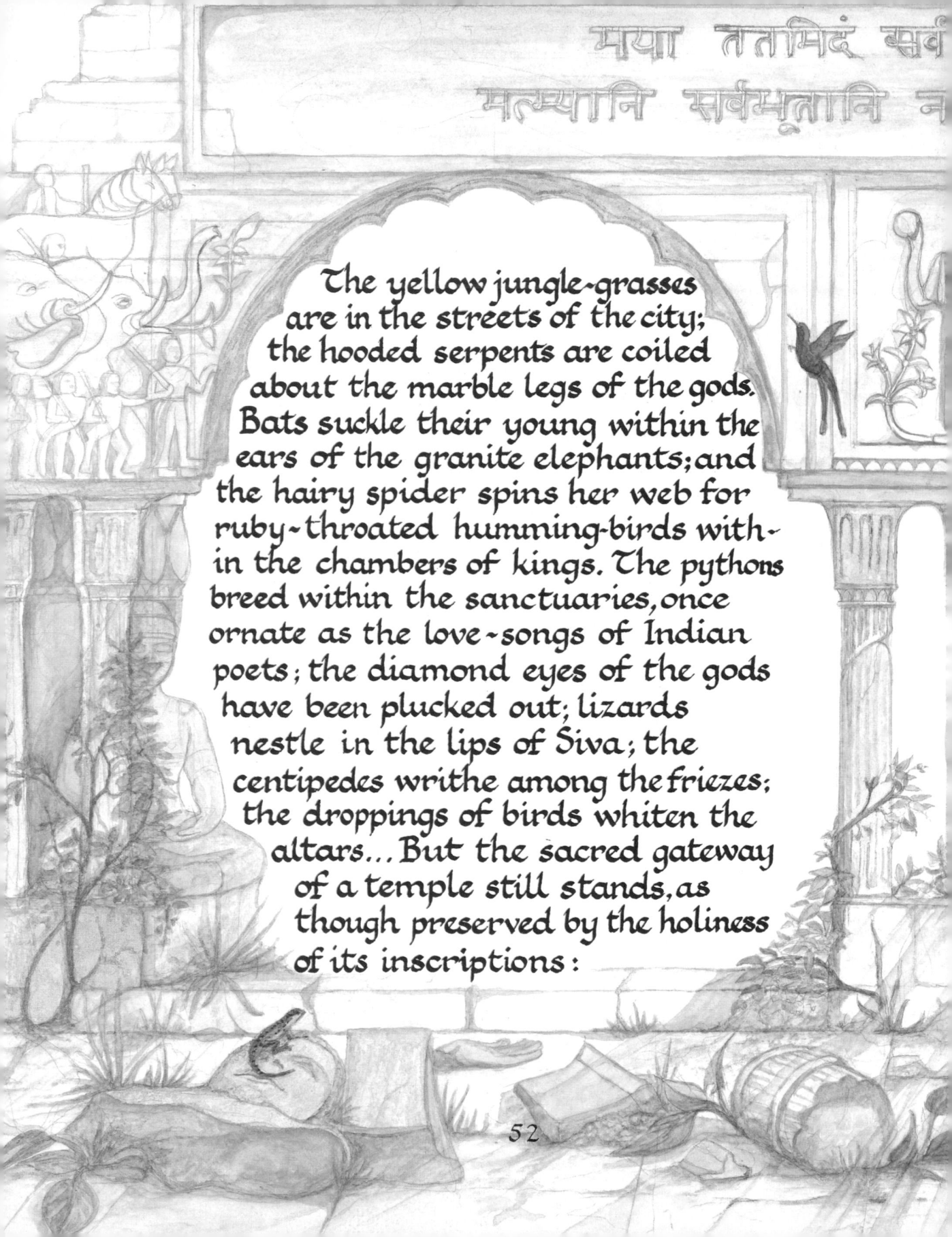

मया ततमिदं सर्व
मत्स्यानि सर्वभूतानि न

The yellow jungle-grasses
are in the streets of the city;
the hooded serpents are coiled
about the marble legs of the gods.
Bats suckle their young within the
ears of the granite elephants; and
the hairy spider spins her web for
ruby-throated humming-birds within the chambers of kings. The pythons
breed within the sanctuaries, once
ornate as the love-songs of Indian
poets; the diamond eyes of the gods
have been plucked out; lizards
nestle in the lips of Siva; the
centipedes writhe among the friezes;
the droppings of birds whiten the
altars... But the sacred gateway
of a temple still stands, as
though preserved by the holiness
of its inscriptions:

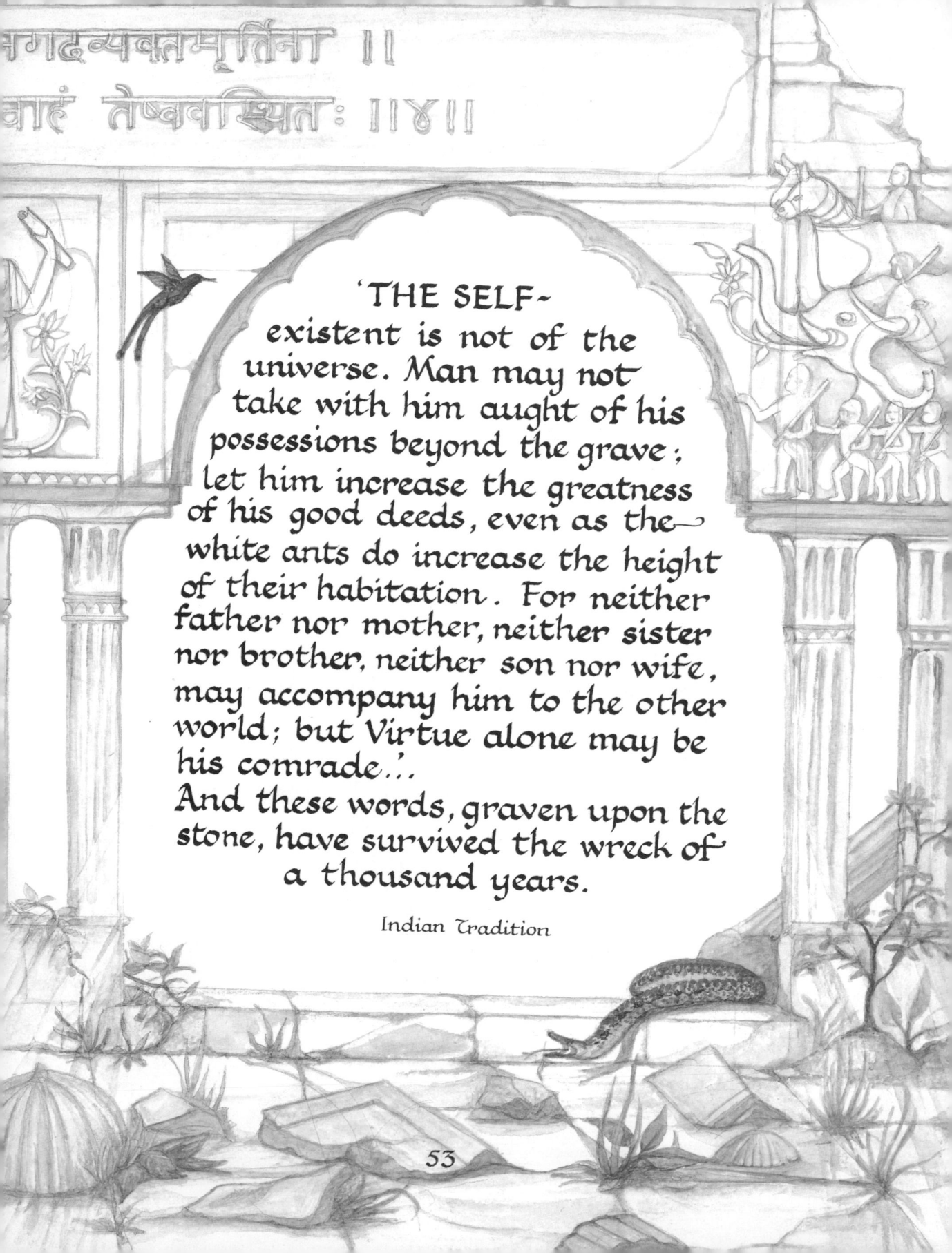

नगढव्यक्तमूर्तिना ॥
वाहं तेष्ववस्थितः ॥५॥

'THE SELF-
existent is not of the
universe. Man may not
take with him aught of his
possessions beyond the grave;
let him increase the greatness
of his good deeds, even as the
white ants do increase the height
of their habitation. For neither
father nor mother, neither sister
nor brother, neither son nor wife,
may accompany him to the other
world; but Virtue alone may be
his comrade...
And these words, graven upon the
stone, have survived the wreck of
a thousand years.

Indian Tradition

53

Where does your pebble walk to,
Grasshopper?
It walks. Its journey is to nowhere.
Each journey begins, and also ends.
Then the ending is the bottom of the pool.
Does not the pebble, entering the water,
begin fresh journeys?
It seems unceasing.

Such is the journey through life.
It begins, it ends, yet fresh journeys go forth.
Grasshopper, when I was a boy I fell into a
hole in the ground and I was broken and
could not climb out. I might have died
there; but a stranger came along and saved
me. He said it was his obligation, that for
help he had once received he must in return
help ten others, each of whom must then
help ten others, so that good deeds would
spread out like the ripples from the pebbles
in a pond. I was one of his ten and you became
one of mine. I pass this obligation on to you.

Oriental Tradition

From the Unreal
      lead us to the Real,
From Darkness
      lead us unto Light,
From Death
      lead us to Immortality.
Reach us through
      and through ourselves
And evermore protect us, ~
O Thou Terrible! ~
      from ignorance
By Thy sweet
      compassionate face.

INDIAN

55

It is a beauteous evening, calm and free;
The holy time is quiet as a Nun
Breathless with adoration; the broad sun
Is sinking down in its tranquillity;

The gentleness of heaven is on the Sea:
Listen! the mighty Being is awake,
And doth with his eternal motion make
A sound like thunder —
                    everlastingly...

W. WORDSWORTH

The day is no more, the shadow is upon
the earth. It is time that I go to the
stream to fill my pitcher.
The evening air is eager with the sad
music of the water. Ah, it calls me out
into the dusk. In the lonely lane there
is no passer by, the wind is up, the
ripples are rampant in the river.
I know not if I shall come back home.
I know not whom I shall chance to
meet. There at the fording in the
little boat the unknown man plays
upon his lute...

RABINDRANATH TAGORE

Now with
its half-disc
leaning
upon some island
the evening sun sets.
The lake is beginning to glow.
There soars the moon from the
rim of the far off sea.
And all my thoughts are
plunged into the hardy
loveliness of autumntide.
Northward I wander in
dreams to Yun, Southward
I search for Yuye...
The lotus is falling,

falling. The river is jewelled with
autumn hues. Long, long the wind blows...
Long, long the night wears!
Fain would I grasp the incredible...
Oh! to fly away seaward and dream for
a little by its shores!
To take from an island in blue ocean the six
                   monsters~
Alas, there is no such length of line.
My hand caresses the surging wind; I am
        deeper drowned in sorrow.
I will away! away! Too strong is the life of
            men for me.
There in the magical land of P'eng Lai
I will gather the grass of immortality.

Li Po

Margaret,
are you grieving
Over Goldengrove unleafing?
Ah! as the heart grows older
It will come to such sights colder
By and by, nor spare a sigh
Tho' world of wanwood leafmeal lie;
And yet you will weep and know why:
Now no matter, child, the name:
Sorrow's springs are the same.
Nor mouth had, no, nor mind express'd,
What heart heard of, ghost guess'd:
It is the blight man
was born for,
It is Margaret you
mourn for.

GERARD MANLEY HOPKINS

Dry those tears, my daughter,
and look upon your Father. Your
Father is the least of all things
in size, just as He is the greatest
of all things in excellence; and
since He is very small He is
within everything, but since
He is very great He is outside
everything. See, I am here with
you, both within and without,
the greatest smallness and the
smallest greatness. Behold, I say,
do you not see? I fill Heaven and
earth. I penetrate and contain them.
                    Marsilio Ficino

THE
ONE
REMAINS,
the many change and pass;
Heaven's light forever shines, Earth's
shadows fly;
Life, like a dome of many-coloured glass,
Stains the white radiance of eternity,
Until Death tramples it to fragments - Die
If thou wouldst be with that which thou
dost seek!
P. B. Shelley

W·E·L·E·A·R·N

one lesson from the seed that diamonds
have never taught us. For seeds, unlike
diamonds, are for spending ~for throwing
away, almost. For unless the seed falls
into the ground, lying buried in the
darkness of the earth for due season,
there can be no spring nor harvest. The
image of the seed is the living message
of truth for all of us: that death of
some kind is the cause of all renewal...

Graham Howe ~

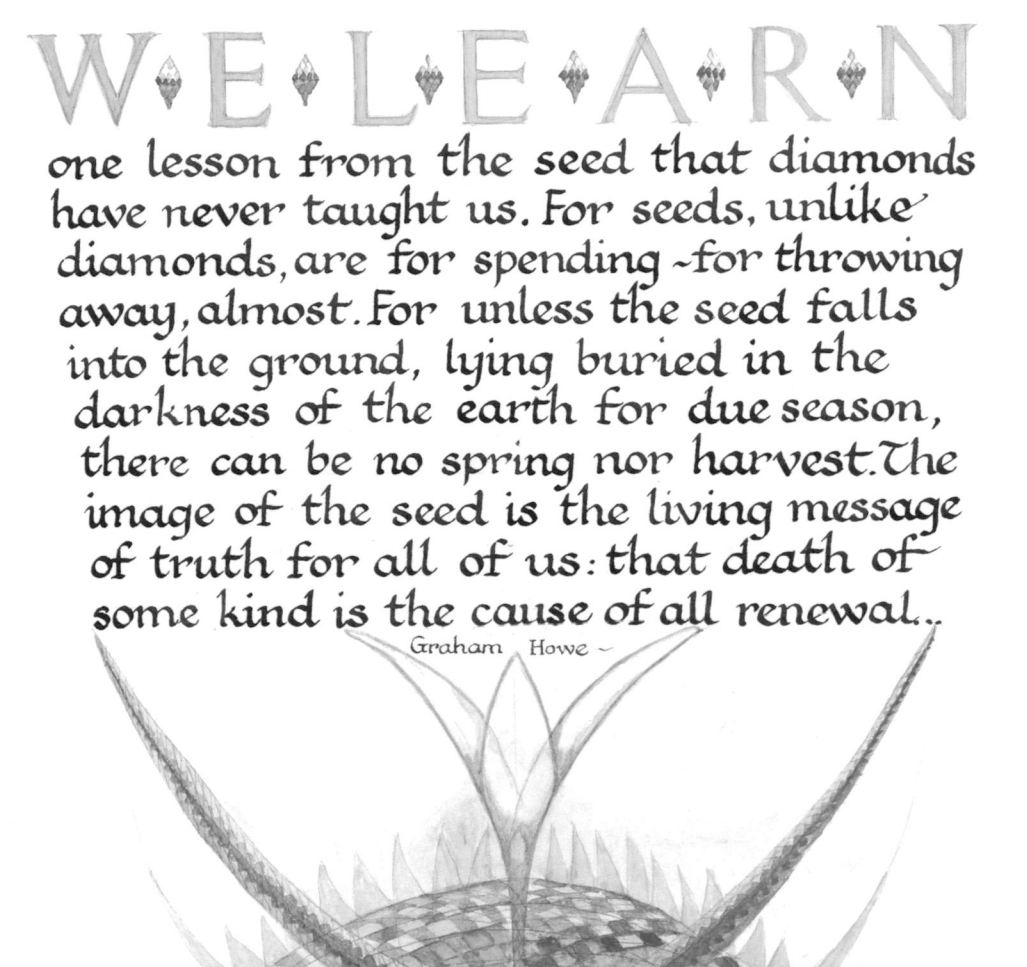

WHERE
WERT THOU
when I laid the
foundations of the
earth? declare if thou
hast understanding?
Who hath laid the measures
thereof, if thou knowest? or who
hath stretched the line upon it?
Whereupon are the foundations thereof fastened or who laid the cornerstone
thereof, when the morning stars sang
together, and all the sons of God
shouted
FOR JOY

BOOK OF JOB

64

I am the wind which blows over the sea,
I am the wave of the ocean; I am the
murmur of the billows,
I am a tear of the Sun, I am the fairest of
plants,
I am a wild boar in valour; I am a salmon
in the water,
I am a lake in the plain...
I am a word of Science; I am the spearpoint
which gives victory;
I am the God which creates in the head of
man the fire of thought.
Who will enlighten each question
if not I?

The Heroic Cycle — Celtic Tradition

And he said: You would know the secret of death.
But how shall you find it unless you seek it in
the heart of life?..
If you would indeed behold the spirit of death,
open your heart wide unto the body of life.
For life and death are one, even as the river
and the sea are one.
In the depth of your hopes and desires lies your
silent knowledge of the beyond;
And like seeds dreaming beneath the snow
your heart dreams of spring.
Trust the dreams,
for in them is
hidden the
gate to
eternity.
Your
fear of
death is
but the
trembling
of the shepherd
when he stands
before the king whose hand is laid upon him
in honour.

Is not the shepherd joyful beneath his trembling,
that he shall wear the mark of the king?
Yet is he not more mindful of his trembling?
For what is it to die but to stand naked in the
wind and to melt into the sun?
And what is it to cease breathing but to free
the breath from its restless tides, that it may
rise and expand and seek God unencumbered?
Only when you drink from the river of silence
shall you indeed sing.
And when you have reached the mountain top,
then you shall begin to climb.
And when the earth shall claim your limbs,
then shall you truly dance.

KAHLIL GIBRAN

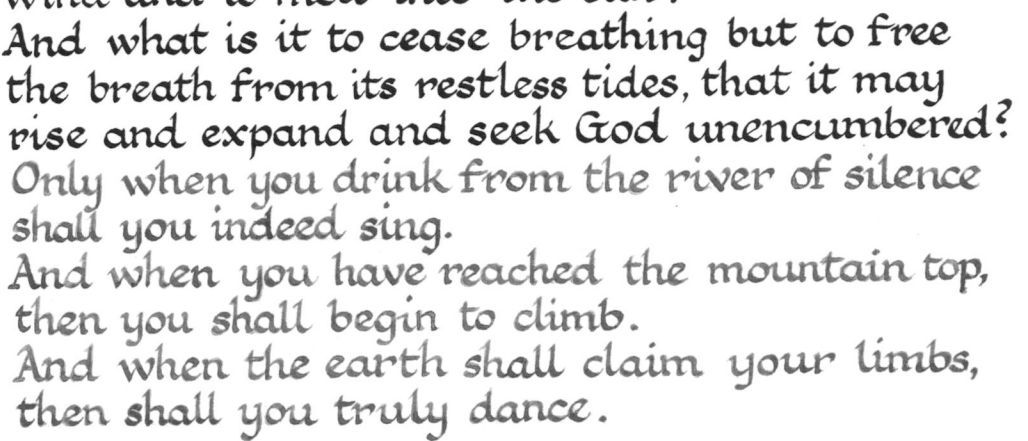

Death is nothing at all; it does not count.
I have only slipped away into the next room.
Nothing has happened; everything remains
exactly as it was. I am I, and you are you,
and the old life that we lived so fondly together is untouched, unchanged. What we were
to each other, that we are still. Call me by the
old familiar name. Speak to me in that easy
way you always used. Put no difference in your
tone. Wear no false air of solemnity or sorrow.
Laugh as we always laughed at the little jokes
that we enjoyed together. Play, smile, think of
me, pray for me. Let my name be ever the
household word that it always was. Let it be
spoken without effort, without the ghost of a
shadow upon it. Life means all that it has ever
meant. It is the same as it always was. There
is absolute and unbroken continuity. What is
this death, but negligible accident? I am but
waiting for you, for an interval somewhere,
very near, just around the corner. All is well.
Nothing is past; nothing is lost. One brief
moment, and all will be as it was before.

CANON HENRY SCOTT~HOLLAND

Master, what is the best way to meet the loss of someone we love?
By knowing that when we truly love, it is never lost. It is only after death that the depth of the bond is truly felt, and our loved one becomes more a part of us than was possible in life.

Are we only able to feel this toward those whom we have known and loved a long time?

Sometimes a stranger, known to us for moments, can spark our souls to kinship for eternity.
How can strangers take on such importance to our souls?
Because our soul does not keep time, it merely records growth.

Love cannot measure itself until the hour of parting. Trust comes from within you. Is not to trust, to rely on someone of whom you know nothing? With each ending comes a new beginning.
I seek not to know all the answers,
but to understand the questions.

Oriental Tradition

For, lo, the

WINTER IS PAST,

the rain is over and gone; the
flowers appear on the earth; the
time of the singing of birds
is come, and the voice of the
turtle is heard in our land.

THE SONG OF SOLOMON

70

THE HUMAN HEART

can go to the lengths of God.
Dark and cold we may be, but this
Is no winter now. The frozen misery
Of centuries breaks, cracks, begins to move;
The thunder is the thunder of the floes,
The thaw, the flood, the upstart Spring.
Thank God our time is now when wrong
Comes up to face us everywhere,
Never to leave us till we take
The longest stride of soul men ever took.
Affairs are now soul size.
The enterprise
Is exploration into God.

CHRISTOPHER FRY

MY life is a tree
Yoke fellow of the earth;
    pledged
By roots too deep for
    remembrance
To stand hard against
    the storm
To fill my place.
(But high in the branches
of my green tree
there is a wild bird
     singing :
Wind~free are the
wings of my bird :
She hath built no
    mortal nest.)

Karle Wilson Baker

O FRIEND

hope in Him while thou livest,
know Him while thou livest,
For in life is thy release.

If thy bonds be not broken while thou livest,
What hope of deliverance in death?

It is but an empty dream that the soul
must pass into union with Him,
Because it hath passed from the body.

If He is found now, He is found then :
If not, we go but to dwell in the city of Death.

If thou hast union now, thou shalt have it
hereafter.

Bathe in the Truth: know the true Master:
Have faith in the true Name.

Kabir saith: It is the spirit of the quest
that helpeth.
I am the slave of the spirit of the quest.

Kabir

Now we should praise the Keeper of the
heavenly kingdom, the Ordainer's might and
his Mind's intent, the works of the Father of
glory: in that He, the eternal Lord, appointed
of every wondrous thing the beginning. He,
the almighty Guardian of mankind, first
created for the sons of men, heaven as a
roof, and afterwards for mortals, the middle-
earth, the world.

CAEDMON

FROM THE POINT OF LIGHT

within the mind of God
Let light stream forth into the minds of men.
Let light descend on earth...

FROM THE CENTRE

which we call the race of men
Let the plan of Love and Light work out
and may it seal the door where evil dwells
Let Light and Love and Power restore
the plan on earth.

TIBETAN TRADITION

DO YOU BELIEVE IN A FUTURE LIFE? he asked.

In a future life? repeated Prince André: but Pierre gave him no time to answer, taking this repetition of his own words for a negation all the more readily because in earlier days he had known the Prince's atheistical convictions.

You say that you cannot see the kingdom of goodness and truth on earth. Neither have I seen it: nor is it possible for any one to see it who looks upon this life as the sum and end of all. On the earth, that is to say on this earth (Pierre pointed to the fields), there is no truth; all is falsehood and evil: but in the universe, in the whole universe, truth has its kingdom; and we who are now children of the earth are none the less children of the universe. Do not I feel in my soul that I am actually a member of this vast harmonious whole? Do not I feel that in this countless assemblage of beings, wherein the Divinity, the First Cause ~ or however you may term it ~ is manifested, I make one link,

one step between the lower beings and the higher?
If I see, and clearly see the ladder leading from
plant to man, then why must I suppose that it
breaks off at me, and does not lead on further
and beyond? I feel not only that I cannot utterly perish, since nothing in the universe is
annihilated, but that I always shall be, and
always was. I feel that besides me are spirits
that live above me, and that in this universe
there is truth.   LEO TOLSTOY

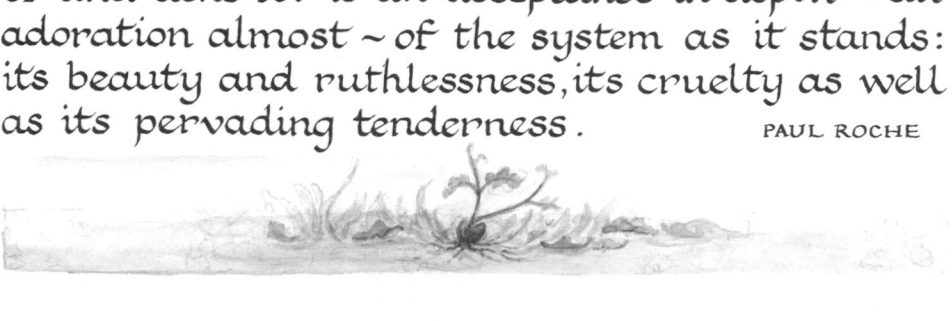

I BELIEVE

that what the whole creational movement tells
of and asks for is an acceptance in depth ~ an
adoration almost ~ of the system as it stands:
its beauty and ruthlessness, its cruelty as well
as its pervading tenderness.   PAUL ROCHE

LORD

make me an instrument
of Thy peace. Where there
is hatred, let me sow love.
Where there is injury, pardon.
Where there is doubt, faith. Where
there is despair, hope. Where there is
darkness, light. Where there is sadness,
joy. O Divine Master, grant that I may
not so much seek to be consoled as to
console; to be understood, as to under~
stand; to be loved, as to love; for it is
in giving that we receive, it is in
pardoning that we are pardoned,
and it is in dying that we
are born to Eternal
LIFE.

ST. FRANCIS OF ASSISI

SPIRIT

of the Living Christ, come upon us in
the glory of Thy risen power.

SPIRIT

of the Living Christ, come upon us in
all the humility of Thy wondrous love.

SPIRIT

of the Living Christ, come upon us that
new life may course within our veins,
new love bind us together in one family.

A NEW VISION

of the Kingdom of God spur us on to
serve Thee with fearless passion.

For Thy sake we ask it. Amen

Prayer from the Iona Community

MESSENGER,

morning brought you
   habited in gold.
After sunset, your song wore a tune of
ascetic grey and then came night.
Your message was written in bright
         letters across the black.
Why is such splendour about you, to
lure the heart of one who is nothing?

Great is the festival hall where
         you are to be the only guest,
Therefore the letter to you is written
         from sky to sky,
And I, the proud servant, bring the
invition with all ceremony.

JNANDAS

80

LOVE bade me welcome; yet
            my soul drew back,
            Guilty of dust and sin.
But quick-eyed Love, observing
            me grow slack
            From my first entrance in,
Drew nearer to me, sweetly questioning
            If I lack'd anything.

'A guest', I answered, 'worthy to be here'.
            Love said, 'You shall be he'.
'I, the unkind, ungrateful? Ah, my dear,
            I cannot look on Thee'.
Love took my hand and smiling did reply,
            'Who made the eyes but I?'

'Truth, Lord, but I have marr'd them:
            let my shame
            Go where it doth deserve'.
'And know you not', says Love, 'who bore
            the blame?'
            'My dear, then I will serve'.
'You must sit down', says Love, 'and taste my meat'.
            So I did sit and eat. George Herbert.

81

Let there be many windows in your soul,
That all the glory of the universe
May beautify it.

Not the narrow pane
Of one poor creed can catch the radiant rays
That shine from countless sources. Tear away
The blinds of superstition; let the light
Pour through fair windows, broad as truth itself
And high as heaven...
... Tune your ear
To all the worldless music of the stars

And to the voice of nature, and your heart
Shall turn to truth and goodness as the plant
Turns to the sun. A thousand unseen hands
Reach down to help you to their peace -
crowned heights,
And all the forces of the firmament
Shall fortify your strength. Be not afraid
To thrust aside half-truths and grasp
the whole.

Ralph Waldo Trine

MEN

seek out retreats for themselves,
cottages in the country, lonely
seashores and mountains. Thou
too art disposed to hanker
greatly after such things: and
yet all this is the very commonest
stupidity; for it is in thy power,
whenever thou wilt, to retire into
thyself: and nowhere is there any
place whereto a man may retire
quieter and more free from politics
than his own soul.

Marcus Aurelius

GIVE

me my scallop ~shell of quiet,
My staff of faith to walk upon,
My scrip of joy, immortal diet,
My bottle of salvation,
My gown of glory, hope's true gage;
And thus I'll take my pilgrimage.

Sir Walter Raleigh

The First Musician

he ancient and valiant
Wainamoinen washed his
thumbs; he purified his
fingers; he seated himself by the
sea upon the Stone of Joy, upon the
Hillock of Silver, even at the summit
of the Hill of Gold; and he took the
instrument within his hands, and
lifted up his voice, saying: "Let him
that hath never heard the strong
joy of runes, the sweet sound of
instruments, the sound of music,
come hither and hear!"
And the ancient Wainamoinen
began to sing. Limpid his voice
as the voice of running water,
deep and clear, mighty
and beautiful...

All the living creatures of the forest, all the
living creatures of the air, drew nigh unto the
rune~singer, gathered themselves about the mighty
chanter, that they might hear the suavity of his
voice, that they might taste the sweetness of his song..
All the heroes wept; the hardest of hearts were
softened ... The youths wept; the old men wept;
the virgins wept; the little infants wept; even
Wainamoinen also felt the source of his own tears
rising to overflow...
They streamed upon his cheeks, and from his
cheeks they fell upon his knees, and from his knees
they dropped upon his feet, and from his feet they
rolled into the dust. And his tear~drops passed
through his six garments of wool, his six girdles
of gold, his seven robes of blue, his eight tunics all
thickly woven.
And the tears of Wainamoinen flowed as a river,
and became a river, and poured themselves to
the shores of the sea, and precipitated them~
selves from the shores into the deeps of the abyss
into the region of black sands.
There did they blossom; there were they trans~
formed into pearls, ~pearls destined for the
crowns of Kings, for the eternal joy of
noblest heroes. From 'The Kalevala'~Finnish Tradition

PEARLS

lie not on the seashore,
If thou desirest one thou must

DIVE

for

it.

Oriental

Proverb

TRUTH

is within ourselves;
it takes no rise
From outward things,
whate'er you may believe.
There is an inmost
centre in us all,
Where truth abides
in fullness.

ROBERT BROWNING

IN meditation it is possible to dive deeper and deeper into the mind to a place where there is no disturbance and there is absolute solitude. It is at this point in the profound stillness that the sound of the mind can be heard. It is like the sea breaking on a far off reef, and it lulls the being into extreme calm. Like the sea it is a music primeval and here is no storm, only the silken waves soughing. When I listen to the sound of this sea, I sense that I am a voyager and this sound is a wind in the sails of a ship. But this sound is not of this world for other sounds are heard distinctly and cause this sound to die, though it returns with the silence. Some-times I think it as a transcendent sound which speaks of unknown powers, of cosmic storms and sun winds sighing in the brain. This is no earthly voyage, and I see visions of ships that sail on no earthly sea. Our ships sail on upon a silent sea; no wind, there is no sound but we move on.

A.E.I. FALCONAR.

At the root of everybody's being there is a tendency to ultimates, to Utopias, to final consummations, to immortality, to God. There is always some incorruptible spiritual atom in us seeking for perfection, creating in us that divine discontent without which the world would be the Devil's world entirely. Out of this incorruptible spiritual atom in the centre of all life arise like an exhalation all the theories about society which men have put forward from time immemorial for the settlement of their troubles. It does not matter whether the theories are practicable or wise or unwise. They all are evidence of the tendency towards final perfection. The right impulse may be deflected by the unequal intellect or the imperfect character of the individual, but all the same if one analyses all the theories of society, however contradictory they are, at the root of them will be found the same impulse and it will appear that all men are really seeking the same end and are journeying together.

THEOSOPHICAL

90

Nothing in the world is single,

All things by a law divine

In one another's being mingle...

Emanuel Schikaneder

I believe in God the Father Almighty because wherever I have looked, through all that I see around me, I see the trace of an intelligent mind, and because in natural laws, and especially in the laws which govern the social relations of men, I see not merely the proofs of an intelligence, but the proofs of beneficence.

Henry George

MAN is, therefore, a noble creation,
as perfect as the scheme
allows; a part of the fabric
of the all, he yet holds
a lot higher than
of all living
things on earth.
~ Plotinus.

MOON follows moon
before the Great Moon
flowers, Moon of the
wild, wild honey that is ours!
Long must the tree strive up
in leaf and root
Before it bear the golden ~
hearted fruit.
And shall great love at
once perfected spring,
Nor grow by steps like
any other thing? Richard le Gallienne

Evil exists not, only the past. The
past is past, the present is the moment.
The future is all. Zoroastra.

ONE DAY

people will touch and talk perhaps easily,
And loving be natural as breathing,
and warm as sunlight;
And people will untie themselves,
as string is unknotted,
Unfold and yawn and stretch and spread
their fingers;
Unfurl, uncurl, like seaweed returned
to the sea.
And work will be simple and swift
like a seagull flying;
And play will be casual and quiet
as a seagull settling.
And the clocks will stop, and no - one
will wonder or care or notice,
And people will smile without reason,
even in the winter,
even in the rain.

A. S. J. Tessimond

MAN'S GREATEST PRIVILEGE IS

to become a suitable instrument of God, and until he knows this he has not realised his true purpose. The whole tragedy in the life of man is his ignorance of this fact. From the moment a man realises this he lives the real life, the life of harmony between God and man. When Jesus Christ said, 'Seek ye first the kingdom of God, and all these things shall be added unto you', this teaching was in answer to the cry of humanity; some were crying 'I have no wealth'; others 'I have no rest', or 'My situation in life is difficult', or 'My friends are troubling me', or 'I want a higher position'. And the answer to them all is what Christ said...

In seeking the kingdom of Heaven we seek the centre of all, both within and without, for all that is in Heaven or on earth is directly connected with the centre.

INAYAT KHAN ~ SUFI ~

Let thy
Soul lend its ear to
every cry of pain like as a
lotus bares its heart to drink
the morning sun. Let not the
fierce Sun dry   one tear of
pain before   thyself hast
wiped it   from the
sufferer's   eye. But let
each burning   human tear
fall on thy   heart and
there remain,   nor ever
brush it off,   until the pain
that caused it is removed. These
tears, O thou of heart most
merciful, these are the streams
that irrigate the fields
of charity
immortal.

VEDIC TRADITION

95

HEAR
O ISRAEL
THE LORD
OUR
G O D
THE LORD IS ONE.

—Jewish Tradition—

I AM THOU
THOU ART I
HE IS OURS
WE BOTH ARE HIS
SO SHALL ALL BE
FOR OUR NEIGHBOUR

G.I. GURDJIEFF

97

MAY He protect us both. May he take pleasure in us both. May we show courage together. May spiritual knowledge shine before us. May we never hate one another. May peace and peace and peace be everywhere.

THE UPANISHADS

BY THE ACCIDENT of good fortune a man may rule the world for a time. But by the virtue of love he may rule the world for E · V · E · R

PHILOSOPHY OF TAO.

98

To love is to know Me,
My innermost Nature,
The truth that I am:
Through this knowledge he enters
At once to my Being.

All that he does
Is offered before Me
In utter surrender.
My grace is upon him,
He finds the eternal,
The place unchanging.

Bhagavad-Gita.~

99

LOVE will teach us all things: but we must learn how to win love; it is got with difficulty: it is a possession dearly bought with much labour and a long time; for one must love not sometimes only, for a passing moment, but always. There is no man who doth not sometimes love: even the wicked can do that. And let not men's sin dishearten thee: love a man even in his sin, for that love is a likeness of the divine love, and is the summit of love on earth. Love all God's creation, both the whole and every grain of sand. Love every leaf, every ray of light. Love the animals, love the plants, love each separate thing. If thou love each thing thou wilt perceive the mystery of God in all: and when once thou perceive this, thou wilt thenceforward grow every day to a fuller understanding of it: until thou come at last to love the whole world with a love that will then be all-embracing and universal. Dostoevsky.

Give Me
your whole heart,
Love and adore Me,
Worship Me always,
Bow to Me only,
And you shall find Me;
This is my promise
Who love you dearly.
Lay down all duties
In Me, your refuge.
Fear no longer
For I will save you
From sin and from
bondage.

Bhagavad - Gita

HEAVEN

above, Heaven below;
Stars above, stars below;
All that is above is also below
Understand this and be

HAPPY

ANCIENT EGYPTIAN

102

Great
is
TRUTH,

and stronger than all things. All the
earth calleth upon Truth, and
the heaven blesseth her; all
works shake and tremble, but
with her is no unrighteous
thing... Truth abideth, and
is strong for ever; she liveth
and conquereth for evermore...
She is the strength, and the king~
dom, and the power, and the majesty,
of all ages.   Blessed be the

GOD
of
Truth.

I   Esdras 4

103

BEHOLD,
the mellow light that floods
the Eastern sky. In signs of praise
both heaven and earth unite. And from
the four-fold manifested Powers a chant of
love ariseth, both from the
flaming Fire and flowing
Water, and from sweet-
smelling Earth and
rushing Wind,
from the deep unfathomable
vortex of that golden
light in which the Victor
bathes, ALL NATURE'S
wordless voice in thousand tones
ariseth to proclaim:
Joy unto ye, O men of Earth.
A Pilgrim hath returned
back from the
other shore.'

HARK!

A CONSCIOUS BEING IS BORN.

VEDIC TRADITION ~

104

ARISE,

shine; for thy light is come,
And the glory of the Lord
is risen upon thee.

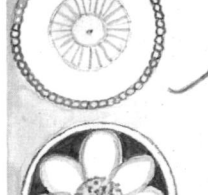

Lift up thine eyes round about, and see:
All they gather themselves together,
they come to thee:

Thy sons shall come from far,
And thy daughters shall be nursed
at thy side.

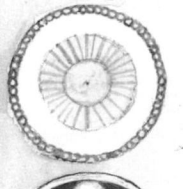

Then thou shalt see, and flow together,
And thine heart shall fear, and
be enlarged...

Thy sun shall no more go down;
Neither shall thy moon
withdraw itself:

For the Lord shall be thine everlasting light,
And the days of thy mourning
shall be ended.

ISAIAH

105

ooked at, but cannot be seen~
That is called the Invisible.
Listened to, but cannot be heard ~
That is called the Inaudible.
Grasped at, but cannot be touched~
That is called the Intangible.
These three elude all our enquiries
And hence blend and become One.

Not by its rising, is there light;
Nor by its setting, is there darkness.
Unceasing, continuous,
It cannot be defined,
And reverts again to the realm
of nothingness.

LAOTSE

GOD

is One and Alone, and there is
none other beside Him. GOD is One
and alone, the Maker of all His creatures.
GOD is a Spirit, deep-hidden from the eye of
man and from all things. GOD is the Spirit
of spirits, of creation the Spirit divine. GOD is
God from the beginning; before all things were
He was God. Lord of existences is He, Father of
all, God eternal. GOD is the One everlasting,
perpetual, eternal, unending. From endless time
hath He been, and shall be henceforth and for
ever. GOD is hidden, and no man His form
hath perceived nor His likeness. Unknown of gods
and of men, mysterious, incomprehensible.
GOD is Truth, and on truth doth He live;
King of truth divine is He. GOD is
life; and man liveth through Him,
the Primeval Alone.

ANCIENT EGYPTIAN

107

Just as the sun is setting there comes a strange quietness and a feeling that everything about you has come to an end...Often it comes most unexpectedly; strange stillness and peace seem to pour down from the heavens and cover the earth. It is a benediction, and the beauty of the evening is made boundless by it...The naked trees, black against the sky, with their delicate branches, were waiting for the spring, and it was just around the corner, hastening to meet them. There was already new grass, and the fruit trees were in bloom. The country was slowly becoming alive again, and from this hill-top you could see the city...You could see the flat tops of the pine trees, and the evening light was upon the clouds. The whole horizon seemed to be filled with these clouds, range after range, piling up against the hills in the most fantastic shapes, castles such as man had never built. There were deep chasms and towering peaks.

All these clouds were alight with a dark red
glow and a few of them seemed to be afire,
not by the sun, but within themselves.
These clouds didn't make the space; they were
in the space, which seemed to stretch infinitely,
from eternity to eternity.
A blackbird was singing in a bush close by, and
that was the everlasting blessing.

KRISHNAMURTI

Only a bell and a bird break the stillness...
It seems that the two talk with the setting sun.
Golden coloured silence, the afternoon is made
                              of crystals.
A roving purity sways the cool trees,
and beyond all that,
a transparent river dreams that trampling
                              over pearls
it breaks loose
and flows into infinity.   JUAN RAMON JIMENEZ

AH! BLESSED LORD!

Oh, high Deliverer!
Ah! Lover! Brother! Guide! Lamp of the Law!
I take my refuge in thy Name and Thee!
I take my refuge in thy law of good!
I take my refuge in thy Order! OM!
The dew is on the lotus! ~ Rise, great Sun!
And lift my leaf and mix me with the wave,
OM MANI PADME HUM,
the sunrise comes!
The dewdrop slips into the shining sea!

LIGHT OF ASIA

INDEX OF AUTHORS
With Dates of Birth and Death, Countries of Birth and First Words.

112

The
GOLDEN
THREAD

This book
belongs to

....
....
....
....
....

D0996376